This book belongs to

_____

I pray for

_____

HARPER BLESSINGS

bee

hand

Bible

light

bird

lips

children

moon

eyes

rain

feet

river

flower

sky

food

sun

grass

world

HARPER BLESSINGS

Everyday Prayers

Edited by Jennifer Frantz

Illustrated by Renée Graef

HarperFestival®
A Division of HarperCollinsPublishers

THIS LITTLE LIGHT

OF MINE

This little of mine,

I'm going to let it shine.

This little of mine—

Hide it under a bushel? Oh, no!

I'm going to let it shine.

Let it shine until Jesus comes!

GOD MADE THE WORLD

God made the

So broad and grand,

Filled with blessings

From His 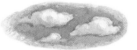 .

He made the

So high and blue,

And all the little

 , too.

FOR FLOWERS THAT BLOOM

For  that bloom

About our ,

For tender ,

So fresh, so sweet,

For song of ,

And hum of ,

For all things fair we hear or see,

Father in heaven,

We thank Thee!

ALL THINGS BRIGHT AND BEAUTIFUL

All things bright and beautiful,

All creatures great and small,

All things wise and wonderful,

The Lord God made them all.

Each little 🌼 that opens,

Each little 🐦 that sings,

He made their glowing colors,

He made their tiny wings.

The purple-headed mountains,

The running by,

The sunset and the morning

That brightens up the .

He gave us to see them,

And that we might tell

How great is God Almighty,

Who has made all things well.

JESUS LOVES ME

Jesus loves me, this I know,

For the  tells me so.

Little ones to Him belong

They are weak, but

He is strong.

I AM THANKFUL

I am thankful for the night

And for the gift of morning .

For rest and ,

For joy and love,

I give thanks to God above.

Help me to be kind and good,

To treat others as I should,

To help the in my own way,

With all I do and all I say.

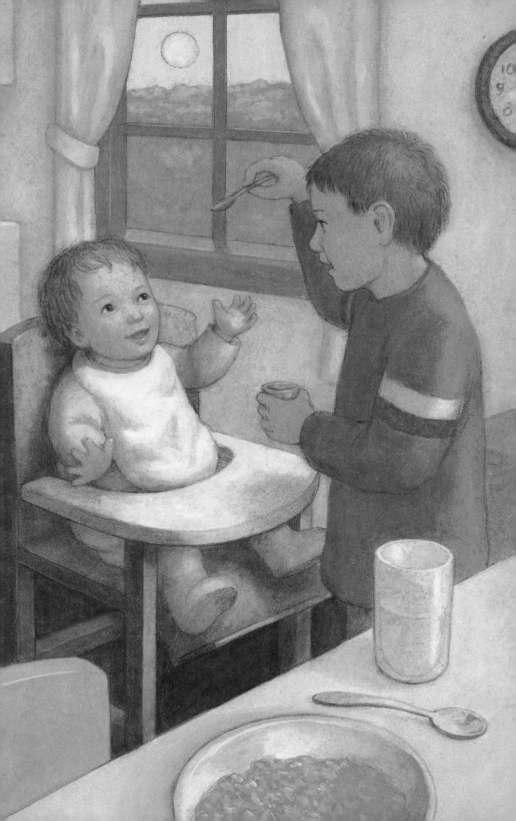

MY BODY, STRONG
AND GOOD

Two that wink and blink.

A mind with which to think.

Two that clap for fun.

Two to jump and run.

Two ears to hear sweet songs.

Two to praise God all day long

I have a body strong and good

To use for Jesus as I should.

HE'S GOT THE WHOLE WORLD

He's got you and me, sister,

in His  .

He's got you and me, brother,

In His .

He's got the wind and the

In His .

He's got the and the

In His .

He's got the whole in His

HERE IS THE CHURCH

Here is the church.

Here is the steeple.

Open the doors.

See all the people!

Close the doors

and hear them pray.

They are thankful

for this day!